4-H Robotics:
Engineering for Today and Tomorrow
Robotics Notebook

Table of Contents

Level 1 — Give Robots a Hand 4

Module 1: Parts Is Parts 5

Module 2: In Arm's Reach 19

Module 3: Get a Grip 28

Level 2 — Robots on the Move 34

Module 1: Get Things Rolling 35

Module 2: Watt's Up? 43

Module 3: Get a Move on 47

Module 4: Under the Sea ROV 54

Level 3 — Mechatronics 60

Module 1: Circuit Training 61

Module 2: Come to Your Senses 69

Module 3: It's Logical 74

Module 4: Do What I Say! 84

Module 5: Ready, SET, Go! 89

4-H Robotics:
Engineering for Today and Tomorrow
Robotics Notebook

Junk Drawer Robotics

The robotic exercises, activities, and use of this notebook will allow you to examine the communication skills that are used by scientists and engineers in technical writing, sketching, and drawing. You will have a chance to practice your own writing and drawing techniques in this 4-H Robotics Notebook. The notebook is a place for you to record your thoughts, ideas, and experiences as you examine the world of robotics. Your notebook should become like a formal diary that you will want to review yourself and share with others. This 4-H Robotics Notebook covers all three levels of the *Junk Drawer Robotics* curriculum. You'll want to continue keeping notes of what you do in all levels and refer back to them often.

Robotics Notebook
Level 1
Give Robots a Hand

In the beginning Junk Drawer Robotics level, "Give Robots a Hand," you will explore the function and design of robotic arms. You will investigate robotic hands, grippers, and other end effectors by studying their movements and power sources.

Module 1 – Parts Is Parts

You will start with activities to practice using your notebook and how to design and communicate like an engineer. As you begin to design and build, you will apply ideas about form and function. You will explore the design, manufacturing, and assembly of items. These objects will then be used to build your own robots.

Module 2 – In Arm's Reach

Module 2 will allow you to examine different robotic arms and their uses. This knowledge will help you design and build a robot arm. You also will study air pressure and its ability to provide power and movement.

Module 3 – Get a Grip

In these activities, you will discover how various end effectors pick up and hold items. This module will conclude when you assemble your robotic arm and hand, and use it to move and grip items using air power!

4-H Robotics:
Engineering for Today and Tomorrow
Robotics Notebook

Date _____

Signature _____

To Learn

Activity A – Think Like a Scientist

Sort all of your items. To fill out the table, count the amount of items you have that fit within that category. Add up your items for totals of each color.

Sorting 1 – Color and Shapes

Color \ Shape	Square	Triangle	Circle	Rectangle	_____	_____	Total
Red							
Blue							
Green							
Yellow							
_____							
_____							

You can take your total data (numbers) above and make a visual chart or graph. Try to make a bar graph or a pie graph using the forms below. How does the data look different in each type?

Graph 1 – Number by Color

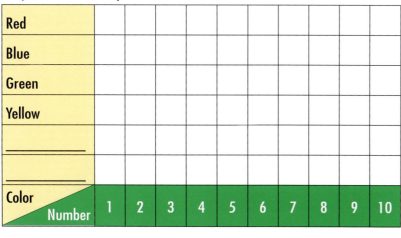

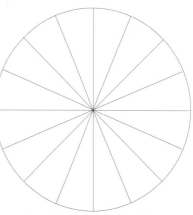

Pie Graph 1A - By Color

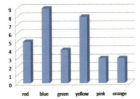
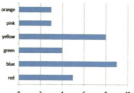

4-H Junk Drawer Robotics • Youth Notebook

4-H Robotics:
Engineering for Today and Tomorrow
Robotics Notebook

Date _____

Signature _____

To Learn

Activity A – Think Like a Scientist

Resort the parts with a different criteria. Then create a new table below that matches your criteria. You can use as many cells as needed; if you need more, draw a new table on a separate sheet.

Sorting 2 – _____

							Total

After resorting all of your objects and filling out the table, use the data to create a graph to visually show the results. Label the graph so others can read the data.

Graph 2 – _____

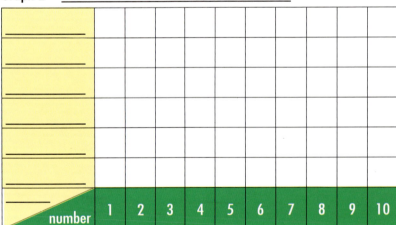

4-H Junk Drawer Robotics • Youth Notebook

4-H Robotics:
Engineering for Today and Tomorrow
Robotics Notebook

Date _____

Signature _____

To Learn

Activity A – Think Like a Scientist

Function –
The purpose of the object; holds things, provides shelter, moves stuff, etc.

Form –
The appearance of the object; how it looks, colors, shapes, materials, etc.

Fill out the table. You should list: the object, its form and its function.

> **Clothespin – Example**
> **Function** – To hold cloth to a wire or cord.
> **Form 1 –**
>   Two pieces of shaped wood
>   One metal wire spring
>   Spring holds wood pieces together
>   Natural wood color
> **Form 2 –**
>   One piece of shaped wood
>   Slot allows pin to slip over cord
>   Natural wood color

Sorting 3 – Form and Function

Item	What is its Function?	What is its Form?

4-H Junk Drawer Robotics • Youth Notebook

4-H Robotics:
Engineering for Today and Tomorrow
Robotics Notebook

Date _____

Signature _____

Activity B – Communicate Like an Engineer – 2-D Drawing

Look around and select an object in the room, but don't let anyone know what it is. Study the item and think about how it looks; pretend you are looking at it from above, at the side of it, and in front of it. Then use the grids below to sketch the object in full detail.

You should draw your object from three different perspectives; the front, side, and top.

Top

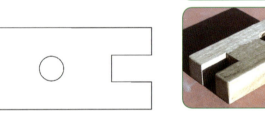

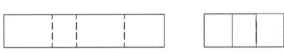

Note how dotted lines were used to show surface changes hidden in some views.

Front

Right Side

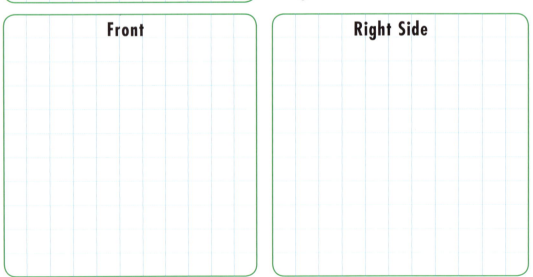

Then exchange your Drawing with the next player so that person can try to locate the same item using your drawing to find the item.

4-H Junk Drawer Robotics • Youth Notebook

4-H Robotics:
Engineering for Today and Tomorrow
Robotics Notebook

Date _____

Signature _____

To Learn

Activity B – Communicate Like an Engineer – Description

After trading notebooks, you will look at the drawing and try to locate the item in the room but not let anyone else know which item it is. Then use the space below to use words to describe that object. Do not use the name of the object in describing the item. Describe the form, not the function of the object. If you do not know what the object is, just describe the object from the pictures drawn by your partner.

Author of Description: _____

Descriptors

Size

Colors

Textures

Shape

Measurements

Patterns

Materials

Surface

Other

Then exchange your Description with the next player. Have that person find the same item using your words to locate the item.

4-H Junk Drawer Robotics • **Youth Notebook**

4-H Robotics:
Engineering for Today and Tomorrow
Robotics Notebook

Date _____

Signature _____

To Learn

Activity B – Communicate Like an Engineer - 3-D Drawing

After trading notebooks with a third member of the group, you will read the Description of the object and then draw a 3-D image of the item. To help, you can use the isometric grid below to line up your 3-D drawing.

Artist _____

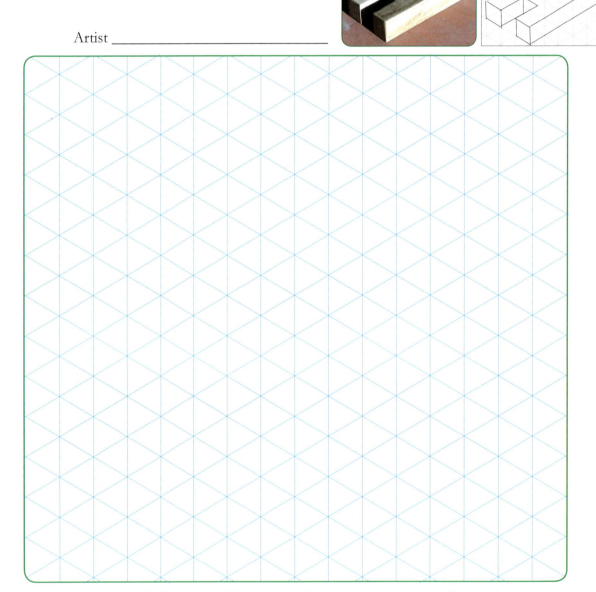

Then exchange your 3-D Drawing with the next player so that person can locate the same item, using your picture drawing to find the item.

10

4-H Junk Drawer Robotics • **Youth Notebook**

4-H Robotics:
Engineering for Today and Tomorrow
Robotics Notebook

Date _____

Signature _____

To Learn

Activity B – Communicate Like an Engineer - Verbal

The fourth and last person in the group will use the 3-D Picture Drawing to locate the item and then will describe the item out loud for people in other groups to guess the item. You can use the area below to make notes for your sharing.

After sharing, return the notebook to its owner and then discuss and make a list of the benefits and problems when using each type of the communication.

Type of Communication	Benefits	Problems
2-D Drawing/Sketch		
Written Description		
3-D Picture Drawing		
Verbal Description		
Other		

Why is it important to have detailed and accurate drawings and descriptions?

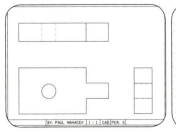 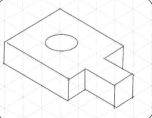 

- Rectangular
- Wooden
- Has a hole through it in the large surface
- Is about 1 inch thick, 3 inches wide, and 5 inches long
- Light tan color
- Smooth surfaces
- One end has a tang

4-H Junk Drawer Robotics • **Youth Notebook**

11

4-H Robotics: Engineering for Today and Tomorrow
Robotics Notebook

CAREER CONNECTIONS

Career Connection 1: Robotics Notebook

Scientists conduct experiments and try to find new knowledge. Engineers apply their knowledge of science, math, and other elements to solve problems. As they work, they need to record their ideas and progress. These notes are usually kept in a notebook. This notebook is an important tool for communication. It records what has been done, what has worked, what has not worked, and ideas about what to work on next. The notebook is also used to assign credit for discoveries, inventions, and patents.

- What type of experiments do you think scientists might work on and record in their notebooks?

- What might an engineer invent or design that would be recorded in a notebook? Engineers use both drawings and words to describe their ideas. Do you think it would be easier for you to use words or drawings to describe a new invention?

4-H Robotics:
Engineering for Today and Tomorrow
Robotics Notebook

Date _____

Signature _____

To Learn

Activity C — Build Like a Technician - Round 1

Building, constructing, and manufacturing are all terms used to describe making items we use. They comprise a set of processes.

We use tools to accomplish most of these tasks (drill, cast, cut, etc.).

How have you used tools to do any of these processes?

Common Manufacturing Processes

Separate – Cut
   Shear
   Turn
   Saw
   Mill

Remove – Shape
   Punch
   Drill
   Sand
   Grind
   Rout

Bend – Form
   Fold
   Seam
   Roll
   Bend
   Forge
   Cast

Join – Fasten
   Glue
   Nail
   Screw
   Weld
   Solder

Building Round 1- Drawing

Basic Square - Using the top, front, and side view drawing (orthographic drawing), construct the drawn item from the parts, craft sticks, and brass brads.

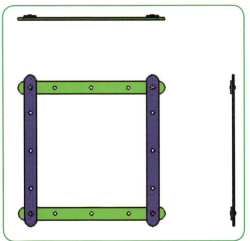

4-H Junk Drawer Robotics • Youth Notebook

13

4-H Robotics:
Engineering for Today and Tomorrow
Robotics Notebook

Date _____

Signature _____

To Learn

Activity C – Build Like a Technician - Round 2

When designing an item, the shapes used are important.

Certain shapes have been found to have special character functions (such as cylinders, triangles, rectangles, arches).

If you look around at things that have been built, you can see some of these shapes.

What shapes can you find in the photos of design shapes? List them below:

Design Shapes
- Triangle
- Diamond
- Rectangle/Square
- Column - Tube
- Arch - Circle

Building Round 2 - Drawing

Basic Triangle - Using the 3-D picture type drawing (isometric), construct the drawn item from craft sticks and paper brads.

Material Shapes
- L - Angle
- I - Beam
- Channel
- Pipe
- Round
- Flat
- Bar
- Board
- Sheet

14

4-H Junk Drawer Robotics • Youth Notebook

4-H Robotics:
Engineering for Today and Tomorrow
Robotics Notebook

Date _____

Signature _____

To Learn

Activity C – Build Like a Technician - Round 3

Building Round 3 - Description

Construct a support to hold a textbook above a tabletop using one sheet of printer paper and four paper clips. The book needs to be at least 5 inches above the tabletop. Use design elements and tools to create your support structure. Below, write about your support structure in your own words and sketch your ideas.

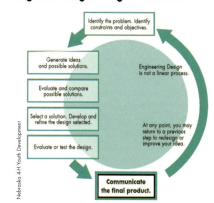

1. The problem/constraints tasks/materials:

2. Sketch many design ideas.

3. List what is good and bad about each design.

Design	Good	Bad

4-H Junk Drawer Robotics • Youth Notebook

4-H Robotics:
Engineering for Today and Tomorrow
Robotics Notebook

Date _____

Signature _____

To Learn

Building Round 3 - Description - continued

4. Select and draw a final design.

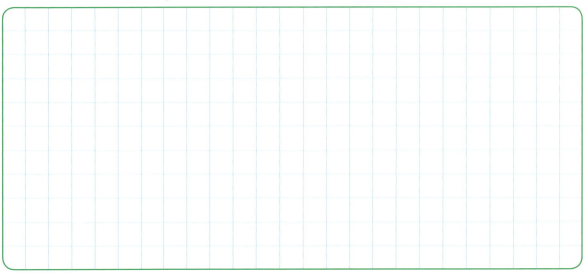

5. Build it; try it out. How did it work?

6. Write about or draw modifications, shapes used, form/function, etc.

4-H Junk Drawer Robotics • Youth Notebook

4-H Robotics:
Engineering for Today and Tomorrow
Robotics Notebook

Date _____

Signature _____

To Do

Activity D – Marshmallow Catapult Design Team

Design a special catapult that can launch a marshmallow:

- Design a "Trebuchet" style swing arm catapult.
- The arm of the catapult must be adjustable (moveable pivot point).
- Use at least five (5) different types of materials or parts (craft sticks, brads, dowels, etc.).
- Use weights and gravity as the power source.
- Launch a marshmallow at least six (6) feet.

Use words, drawings, measurements, and other tools to help in describing your design. Describe the materials you plan to use and how you may have to change them by cutting, bending, or fastening them together.

4-H Junk Drawer Robotics • Youth Notebook

4-H Robotics:
Engineering for Today and Tomorrow
Robotics Notebook

Date _____

Signature _____

To Make

Activity E – Marshmallow Catapult Build Team

Describe how your design worked and any changes you had to make since your first design.

Indicate the target pattern for your marshmallow landings. Were they 6 feet away; were they close to each other?

Draw your final design below:

4-H Robotics:
Engineering for Today and Tomorrow
Robotics Notebook

Date _____

Signature _____

To Learn

Activity F – Sense of Balance

In a balanced state:

Torque = Force x Distance

Torque on left side = Torque on right side

Example:

6 washers x 2 holes = 4 washers x 3 holes
6 x 2 = 4 x 3
12 = 12

Leverage is important.

We can use beams of different lengths to control our robot arm movements.

	Sense of Balance Data Sheet							
	Left Side			Balanced	Right Side		
	Weight (Number of Washers)	**Distance** (Pivot to Washers) (Inches)	**Torque** (Weight x Distance)	=	**Weight** (Number of Washers)	**Distance** (Pivot to Washers) (Inches)	**Torque** (Weight x Distance)
Example	4	3	12	=	6	2	12
1				=			
2				=			
3				=			
4				=			
5				=			
6				=			
7				=			
8				=			

When you change the pivot point on the balance beam, what happens?

Describe some common levers we use.

What levers are similar to the one you made?

4-H Robotics:
Engineering for Today and Tomorrow
Robotics Notebook

Date _____

Signature _____

To Learn

Activity G – ABC ... XYZ

3-D Tic-Tac-Toe Game Instructions:

Play begins by having each team take turns to spin and get three coordinate numbers (X, Y, Z).

Each team records their X, Y, and Z numbers on the scorecard.

The team then finds the 3-D location on the 3-D stand and places one of its game pieces on that spot.

Play continues with each team spinning and marking its 3-D location.

The goal is to get team markers to align in a straight line.

How many points would it take to make a straight line?

What are the different ways to make a straight line in the game?

What would happen if there were more points (4 or 5 or 6) on the grid?

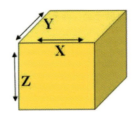

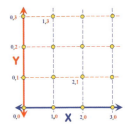

Team Name: _____

Turn	X	Y	Z
Spin 1			
Spin 2			
Spin 3			
Spin 4			
Spin 5			
Spin 6			
Spin 7			
Spin 7			
Spin 8			
Spin 9			
Spin 10			
Spin 11			
Spin 12			
Spin 13			
Spin 14			
Spin 15			

4-H Robotics:
Engineering for Today and Tomorrow
Robotics Notebook

CAREER CONNECTIONS

Career Connection 2: Attributes of an Engineer

Being an engineer requires specific knowledge and skills, above and beyond just training in engineering fields. While engineers must have a good understanding of basic scientific knowledge, including mathematics, physical and life sciences, and information technology, they also need to be curious, creative, and have a desire to learn.

Engineers need to be well-rounded and understand the social context of their issue, including the history, economics, and environment relating to the problem. Basic knowledge of science and society provides engineers with a foundation for approaching potential solutions that will work best in the real world.

In addition, engineers often have many natural characteristics that prepare them well for their career. Engineers need to understand the importance of teamwork and the ability to work with others. Engineers must be patient and flexible. They should have sound ethics, good communication skills (written, verbal, and graphics), and have safe work practices. These traits, combined with their formal education, help engineers to work effectively when devising innovative solutions.

- Which of these life skills do you possess? Which do you need to improve?
- In your opinion, what is the most important skill for an engineer? Why?

4-H Robotics:
Engineering for Today and Tomorrow
Robotics Notebook

Date _____

Signature _____

To Do

Activity H – Arm in Arm Design Team

Design a robot arm that will:

- Use levers or linear movement.
- Pick up a weight.
- Move in two of the three coordinate directions:
  - X (side to side)
  - Y (in and out)
  - Z (up and down).

Design your robot arm below:

4-H Robotics:
Engineering for Today and Tomorrow
Robotics Notebook

Date _____

Signature _____

To Make

Activity 1 – Arm in Arm Build Team

What problems did you encounter when you were building the arm?

What worked well?

Describe what you observed during this activity.

What are the different types of robot arms and how do they work/move?

List any changes you made since your first design.

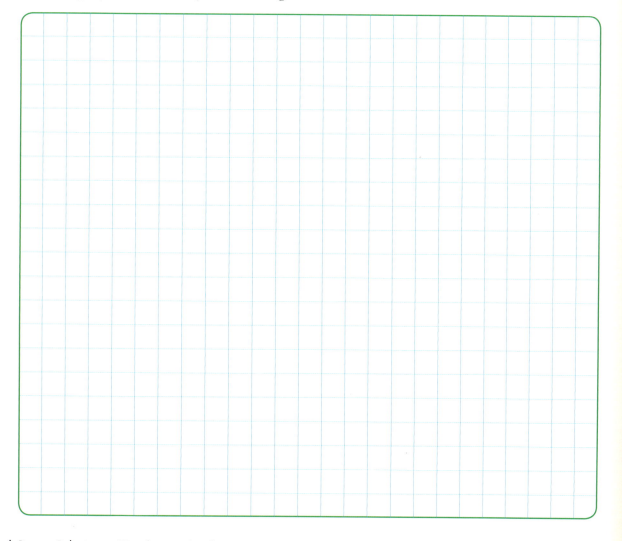

4-H Junk Drawer Robotics • Youth Notebook

4-H Robotics:
Engineering for Today and Tomorrow
Robotics Notebook

Date _____

Signature _____

To Learn

Activity J – Pumped Up

Which bottles successfully turned the pinwheel?
Which didn't?

Which ones worked the best?

How is this example like the wind?

What is the difference between a closed and an open system?

How can we use controlled air (pneumatics) to lift items?

4-H Robotics:
Engineering for Today and Tomorrow
Robotics Notebook

Date _____

Signature _____

To Do

Activity K – Just Add Air Design Team

Your robot arm must:

- Accomplish the task using air power, without direct hand movement by the team.
- Use plastic syringes and tubing for air power.
- Lift a weight.
- Be able to move in two of the three coordinate directions:
  – X (side to side)
  – Y (in and out)
  – Z (up and down).

Design your robotic arm below:

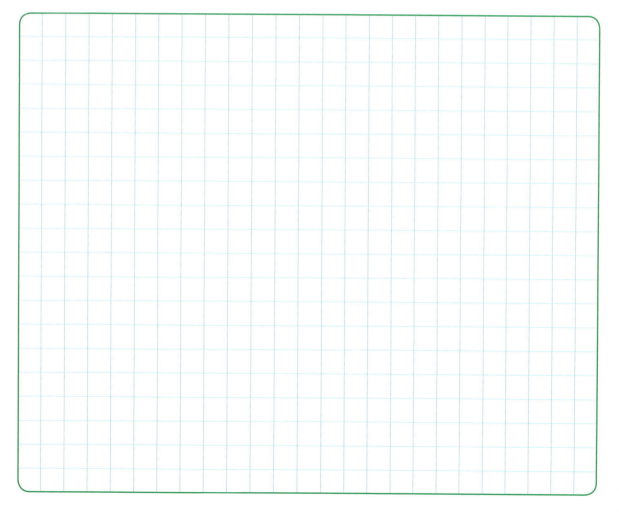

4-H Junk Drawer Robotics • **Youth Notebook**   25

4-H Robotics:
Engineering for Today and Tomorrow
Robotics Notebook

Date _____

Signature _____

To Make

Activity L – Just Add Air Build Team

When you added air power, what was difficult and what worked well?

How did the arm move (smooth, jerky)?

What other parts might make it easier to move this robot arm?

What changes did you make in your design?

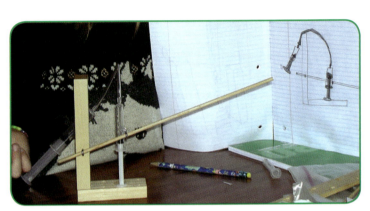

4-H Robotics:
Engineering for Today and Tomorrow
Robotics Notebook

Date _____

Signature _____

To Learn

Activity M – Chopsticks

Where is the pivot joint of your chopsticks?

How were your chopsticks effective?

What was difficult about holding onto the objects? What was easy?

Design a chart to list the items you tried to pick up and list if it was easy or hard to pick them up.

4-H Robotics:
Engineering for Today and Tomorrow
Robotics Notebook

Date _____

Signature _____

To Learn

Activity N – Just a Pinch

Which item(s) did you pick up? Describe the pivot, lever, fulcrum, etc.

How might a robot hand need to be adapted for different items?

Describe several different types of grippers.

4-H Robotics:
Engineering for Today and Tomorrow
Robotics Notebook

Date _____

Signature _____

To Learn

Activity O – Hold On

What item do you have?

Make a list of grippers that you think would work well to hold this item.

How did testing the grippers change your predictions?

How are the structures of grippers related to their functions?

Draw the gripper that best picked up your object:

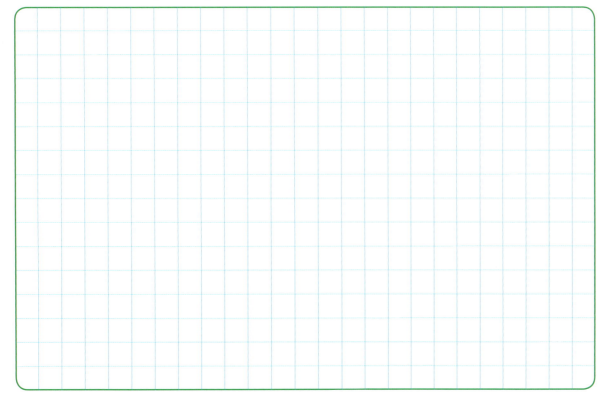

4-H Junk Drawer Robotics • Youth Notebook

29

4-H Robotics:
Engineering for Today and Tomorrow
Robotics Notebook

Date _____

Signature _____

To Do

Activity P – One for the Gripper Design Team

Your robot gripper must:

- Use material from the Trunk of Junk.
- Use air power to move without hand movements from the team.
- Be able to grip and lift a lightweight object.

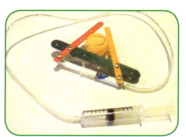

Design your robot gripper below:

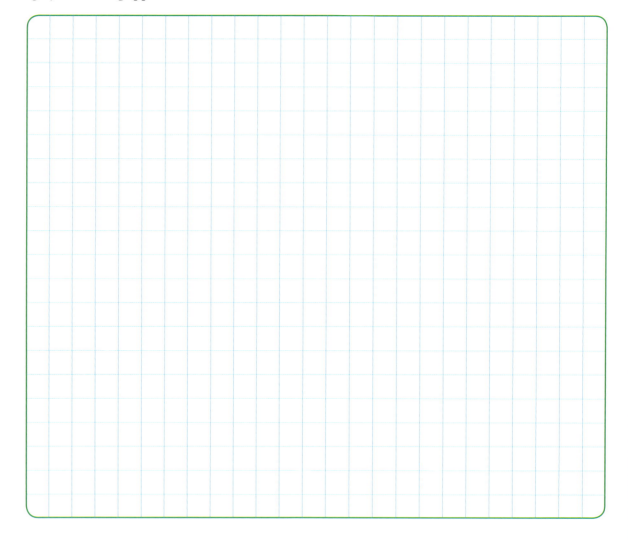

30

4-H Junk Drawer Robotics • **Youth Notebook**

4-H Robotics:
Engineering for Today and Tomorrow

Date _____

Signature _____

To Make

Activity Q – One for the Gripper Build Team

How were you able to attach your gripper to a robotic arm?

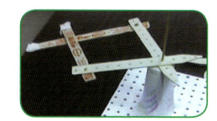

What were some of the linkages used in the gripper?

How did the gripper work to pick up an object?

How easy was it for the gripper to lift objects it wasn't designed to grab? Why? Were the objects similar in size, shape, weight, or material?

List any changes you've made since your first design.

4-H Junk Drawer Robotics • Youth Notebook

4-H Robotics:
Engineering for Today and Tomorrow
Robotics Notebook

Date _____

Signature _____

To Do

Activity R – Twist of the Wrist Design Team

Design a wrist to attach your gripper to your robotic arm:

- Use one of the wrist movements such as: yaw, bend (pitch), or rotation (roll).
- Make sure the wrist has at least one degree of freedom.

Design your wrist below:

4-H Robotics:
Engineering for Today and Tomorrow
Robotics Notebook

Date _____

Signature _____

To Make

Activity 5 – Twist of the Wrist Build Team

As you look at your robot arm and others

What are some ways that worked to attach the gripper?

How did the differences in arm size, leverage, or gripper size affect the attachment and use of the total robot arm and gripper?

How could you add more wrist movements?

4-H Junk Drawer Robotics • Youth Notebook   **33**

4-H Robotics:
Engineering for Today and Tomorrow
Robotics Notebook

Robotics Notebook
Level 2

Robots on the Move

In this second level of Junk Drawer Robotics, you will learn about the forces that enable robots to move. You will explore friction, electrical power, and mechanical structures. These components will be put to the test as you design and build your own robot.

Module 1 – Get Things Rolling

Module 1 will introduce you to the different types of friction. By observing friction's effect on an object's motion, you will learn that it is a large component of robotic engineering. You will then design and build you own friction-minimizing robot.

Module 2 – Watts Up

In Module 2, you will explore the use of electrical power. These exercises will introduce you to electromagnetic fields, electrical circuits, and electric motors. This new knowledge will help you understand how some robots are powered.

Module 3 – Get a Move On

This module will allow you to discover the mechanical aspects of robots. You will learn about gears, axles, and switch controls. Using your new knowledge of gears, you will build your own slow-moving rover.

Module 4 – Under the Sea ROV

In this module, you will explore buoyancy and create an underwater robot or Remotely Operated Vehicle (ROV). Will it sink or float?

4-H Robotics:
Engineering for Today and Tomorrow
Robotics Notebook

Date _____

Signature _____

To Learn

Activity A – Slip N Slide

Test sliding the box of paper clips on the control section of plain cardboard and then on slick tape, sandpaper, and other surfaces for comparisons.

Test by slowly raising the angle of the cardboard ramp until the box of paper clips begins to slide down the ramp.

Measure the angle at which the box of paper clips begins to move. Repeat to get an average angle.

Predictions

Which surface will have the least friction?

1 _____

2 _____

3 _____

4 _____

Surface	Test #	Angle when box began to move
Control Surface Plain Cardboard Ramp	#1	
	#2	
	#3	
Surface A	#1	
	#2	
	#3	
Surface B	#1	
	#2	
	#3	
Surface C	#1	
	#2	
	#3	
Surface D	#1	
	#2	
	#3	

What had the greatest effect on friction?

Why do you think it's important to repeat the same experiment?

Why is it important to do a control?

4-H Junk Drawer Robotics • **Youth Notebook**

4-H Robotics:
Engineering for Today and Tomorrow
Robotics Notebook

Date _____

Signature _____

To Learn

Activity B – Rolling Along

Put your box of paper clips on rollers!

Create axles and cylinder rollers using paper clips and pieces of straws.

Test the rollers just like you did for sliding the box in Activity A.

Box with Rollers

Predictions

Which surface will have the least friction?

1 _____

2 _____

3 _____

4 _____

Surface	Test #	Angle when box began to move
Control Surface Plain Cardboard Ramp	#1	
	#2	
	#3	
Surface A	#1	
	#2	
	#3	
Surface B	#1	
	#2	
	#3	
Surface C	#1	
	#2	
	#3	
Surface D	#1	
	#2	
	#3	

Where have you heard about using rollers to move heavy objects?

Describe your experience of making axles and cylinders.

Which moved first, the box with rollers or the one with the plain bottom surface? Why?

4-H Robotics: Engineering for Today and Tomorrow
Robotics Notebook

CAREER CONNECTIONS

Career Connection 3: Constraints

There are many elements for engineers to consider when approaching a problem. Oftentimes, there are constraints that impact the engineering design process, especially in the type of design that can realistically be built. Engineers use their creativity and resources to overcome these obstacles.

Engineers must take time into account when devising a solution, because they often work on a deadline. "Time to market" is used to describe the time needed to plan, create, test, produce, and release a new product. The timely delivery of products to people is critical for companies to profit. To minimize their "time to market," engineers work in teams, sometimes assigned to specialized components of the overall product.

Money is another constraint that engineers face. Engineers constantly search for less expensive materials that perform similarly to their expensive counterparts. Along with the expense of resources, engineers also must consider the availability of these materials. Certain supplies are sometimes unavailable, so engineers must find replacements and alternative equipment.

The physical elements of components also pose a challenge. Engineers must use physics and mathematics to ensure that the dimensions of their device will allow it to function correctly. They must find materials with properties that best suit the design.

- What are some constraints that you face in daily life? What are some ways you have found to work within those constraints?
- What do you think are some of the constraints in building a robot? Why?

4-H Robotics:
Engineering for Today and Tomorrow
Robotics Notebook

Date _____

Signature _____

To Do

Activity C – Clipmobile Design Team

Customer Requirements for a Clipmobile:

- Design a vehicle that will overcome friction and roll freely down a ramp, and travel a long distance. (performance)
- It must be able to carry a box of paper clips. (capacity)
- It must contain at least five different types of parts. (complexity)
- It must use the least total number of all parts. (efficiency)
- Cost target is to be no more than $35.00 of play money, including start-up supplies in inventory bag. (budgeting)

Manufacturing Selection Criteria

Criteria to select the team that will be chosen to mass produce the Clipmobile:

Meeting Design Criteria (constraints)

Capacity – carry a box of paper clips: (Yes) 10 points; (No) 0 points _____

Performance – roll down ramp and coast: +1 point per inch – maximum 24 points _____

Complexity – various types of parts used: +2 points for each type of part _____

Efficiency – least overall number of parts: -1 point for each part used _____

Budget/cost – cost of production: +1 point for each dollar under $35.00 _____

-2 points for each dollar over $35.00 _____

Team Business Strength

Capital – dollars left from $45.00   +1 point for each dollar still in cash _____

Inventory value – value of supplies in inventory   +1 point for each dollar of value _____

Overall Team Score _____

38   4-H Junk Drawer Robotics • Youth Notebook

4-H Robotics:
Engineering for Today and Tomorrow
Robotics Notebook

Date _____

Signature _____

To Do

Activity C – Clipmobile Design Team

Junk Drawer Supply Company

JDSC is the official supplier of all materials for Clipmobile design, development, and manufacturing. Thank you for using JDSC.

How to get parts and supplies:

1. The Junk Drawer Supply Company will provide each Design Team with a Materials Order Form (MOF) and a sample of the different items for sale. This sample pack of supplies will only cost $10.00 for the whole bag of supplies (Over a $25.00 value of supplies — what a bargain!). These items can be used in your design process and in your building activity.

2. During the *Design*, complete the MOF, listing the total number of each part or item you plan to use.

3. Calculate the cost for each type of part you have ordered.

4. Add up all the costs for parts to get the total dollar amount needed to purchase all the items.

5. During the *Build activity*, have one of your team members take the completed MOF to the Junk Drawer Supply Company area to pay for and pick up the materials ordered.

6. The Junk Drawer Supply Company has limited operating hours and will close after all the teams have filled their orders. Make sure to order enough to build your Clipmobile, but try not to have too many extras as leftover inventory is only worth half of its cost new.

7. The Junk Drawer Supply Company is very picky and will not accept any returned parts or items.

Junk Drawer Supply Company
Clipmobile Materials Order Form (MOF)

	Sold to:			Order Date
Item Code #	**Item/Part Description**	**Price per Item**	**Number Ordered**	**Total Cost (Price X Number)**
101	Craft Stick – Large or small	$3.00		
102	Craft Stick *w/holes* – Large or small	$4.00		
203	Paper Clip – Large or small	$1.00		
304	Brass Paper Brad – Various sizes	$1.00		
405	Binder Clip – Various sizes	$2.00		
506	Drinking Straw – Various sizes	$2.00		
507	Coffee Stirrer Straw	$1.00		
608	Rubber Band – Various sizes	$1.00		
709	Wheel – Various sizes	$3.00		
810	Wood Skewer – Various sizes	$2.00		
Thanks for using **Junk Draw Supply Company**. See us first for all your robot supplies!			**Grand Total:**	

4-H Junk Drawer Robotics • Youth Notebook

4-H Robotics:
Engineering for Today and Tomorrow
Robotics Notebook

Date _____

Signature _____

To Do

Activity C – Clipmobile Design Team

Using the sample pack of parts from the JDR Supply Company, design your Clipmobile below.

Once you determine the parts and quantity needed for your design, complete the Materials Order Form (MOF) and purchase your items.

4-H Robotics:
Engineering for Today and Tomorrow
Robotics Notebook

Date _____

Signature _____

Activity D – Clipmobile Build Team

Use your design and the materials you "purchased" to build your Clipmobile.

- Test that it can hold a box of paper clips.
- Test that it can roll down the ramp.
- Measure how long it would roll carrying the box of paper clips.

What difficulties did you find in building your Clipmobile?

What were the problems of staying on budget?

Figure the cost to build one Clipmobile using the COP report.

Calculate the cost of production for 100 cars.

Clipmobile Report
Cost of Production (COP)

Date of Production: _____   Location of Mfg.: _____   Manufactured by: _____

Item Code #	Item/Part Description	Price Per Item	Number Used in Vehicle*	Total Cost (Price X Number)	Check Items Used in This Build
101	Craft Stick – Large or small	$3.00			
102	Craft Stick *w/ holes* – Large or small	$4.00			
203	Paper Clip – Large or small	$1.00			
304	Brass Paper Brad – Various sizes	$1.00			
405	Binder Clip – Various sizes	$2.00			
506	Drinking Straw – Various sizes	$2.00			
507	Coffee Stirrer Straw	$1.00			
608	Rubber Band Various sizes	$1.00			
709	Wheel – Various sizes	$3.00			
810	Wood Skewer – Various sizes	$2.00			
*include full value even if only part of an item was used, cut in half, taken apart, etc.		Totals			
			Total Parts Used	Total Cost of Production	Total Parts Used

4-H Junk Drawer Robotics • Youth Notebook

4-H Robotics:
Engineering for Today and Tomorrow
Robotics Notebook

Date _____

Signature _____

To Make

You may have some parts left over that you did not use or parts that you cut or bent, or that broke when working on them.

Sort these extra parts into two stacks: one stack is good parts that could be used in a different activity and the second stack is the broken, bent, or used parts that are not like new.

Since the first stack is good as new, take an inventory (count) of them and record it on the Materials Inventory Sheet (MIS).

Clipmobile Report
Materials Inventory Sheet (MIS)
List of supplies left over and in good condition | For office use only

Date of Inventory: _____ | Location of Mfg.: _____ | Name of Manufacturer: _____

Item Code #	Item/Part Description	Used Value Per Item	Number of Good Items Still on Hand*	Total Value (Price X Number)	Verification of Inventory on Hand
101	Craft Stick – Large or small	$1.50			
102	Craft Stick w/holes – Large or small	$2.00			
203	Paper Clip – Large or small	$0.50			
304	Brass Paper Brad – Various sizes	$0.50			
405	Binder Clip – Various sizes	$1.00			
506	Drinking Straw – Various sizes	$1.00			
507	Coffee Stirrer Straw	$0.50			
608	Rubber Band Various sizes	$0.50			
709	Wheel – Various sizes	$1.50			
810	Wood Skewer – Various sizes	$1.00			
*only include complete items in good usable condition; not those cut, drilled, bent, taken apart, etc.		Totals			
			Total Parts Not Used	Total Value of Parts on Hand (Inventory)	

List any changes and modifications you've made since your first design.

4-H Robotics:
Engineering for Today and Tomorrow
Robotics Notebook

Date _____

Signature _____

To Learn

Activity E – Light Up My Life

Using a battery, aluminum foil, and a light bulb, create a circuit that will light up the bulbs.

Below, draw your configurations that worked or didn't work.

Did the battery or wire heat up? If so, why do you think this happened?

4-H Junk Drawer Robotics • Youth Notebook

4-H Robotics:
Engineering for Today and Tomorrow
Robotics Notebook

Date _____

Signature _____

To Learn

Activity F – Magnetic North

What happened with the paper clips and the compass when you used a single straight wire in the circuit?

What changed when you used a coiled wire in the circuit?

Why do you think there is a difference in the straight and coiled wires? How do you think electricity and magnetism are related?

Draw and describe how you think a motor uses magnetism to move.

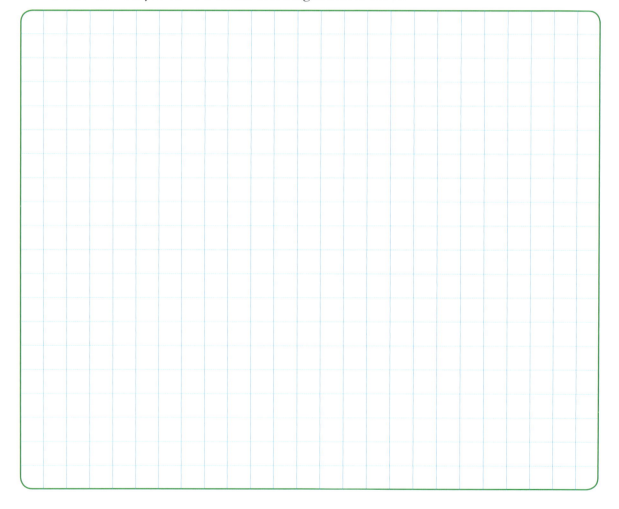

44

4-H Junk Drawer Robotics • **Youth Notebook**

4-H Robotics:
Engineering for Today and Tomorrow
Robotics Notebook

Date _____

Signature _____

To Do

Activity G – Can-Can Robot Design Team

Design a Can-Can Robot that will draw on a sheet of paper using only

- a cup,
- toy motor,
- a battery,
- rubber bands,
- a pencil eraser,
- felt pens, and
- masking tape.

Design your Can-Can Robot below.

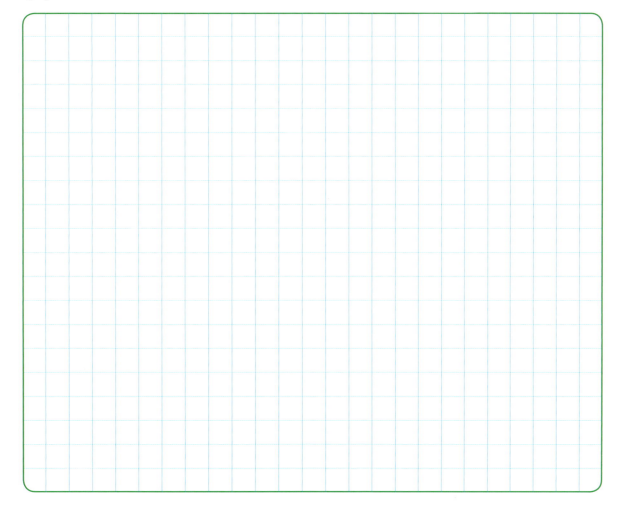

4-H Junk Drawer Robotics • Youth Notebook

45

4-H Robotics:
Engineering for Today and Tomorrow
Robotics Notebook

Date _____

Signature _____

To Make

Activity H – Can-Can Robot Build Team

Record your experience by writing notes, drawing designs, or making charts.

Did your robot draw? What did its drawings (markings) look like?

What aspects of your design worked well?

What could have been improved?

How could you change what your robot can draw?

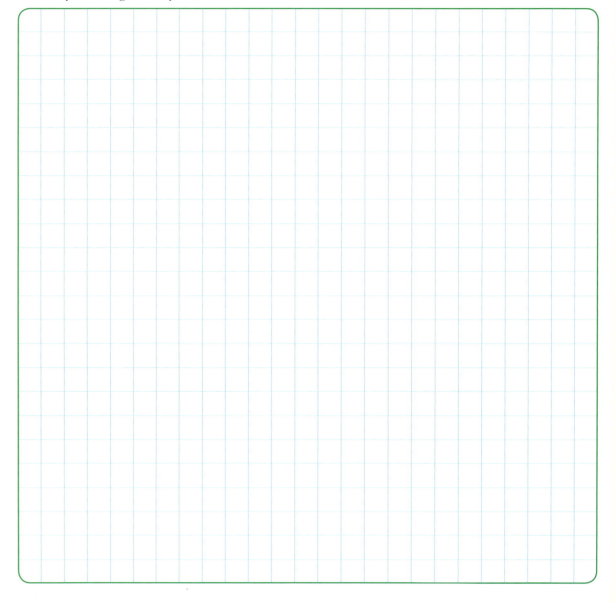

4-H Robotics:
Engineering for Today and Tomorrow
Robotics Notebook

Date _____

Signature _____

To Learn

Activity 1 – Gear We Go Again

Play a game acting like gears.

What happened when you used different sizes of groups for the gear game?

What did you notice about the direction and speed of each group as they rotated?

Why do some bikes, cars, tractors, and other equipment use different gear ratios?

How would a gear ratio affect riding in different conditions?

Count rotations and the number of teeth on each gear (sprocket) to determine the ratio for each "speed" setting.

Gear Ratios

Counting Rotations

Rotation of driver : Rotation of driven
Peddle Crank 1 turn : Rear Wheel 3 turns
1:3 ratio

Counting Teeth

Driven gear divided by Driver gear
wheel sprocket divided by crank sprocket
18 divided by 54
18/54
1/3 = 1:3 ratio

4-H Junk Drawer Robotics • Youth Notebook

Date _____

Signature _____

To Learn

Activity J – Gears and More Gears

Design a gear train:

- That has at least three gears.
- That has a ratio of at least 3:1.
- Has the driver gear and driven gear spinning in opposite directions.

To calculate gear ratio:

Driven Gear divided by **Driver Gear**

Driver Gear # of Teeth	Driver Gear # of Teeth	Calculated Gear Ratio	Observed Gear Ratio

What do you think gears might be used for?

In what tools or machines have you seen gears used? How are they used?

What are different limitations to a gear train?

48

4-H Robotics:
Engineering for Today and Tomorrow
Robotics Notebook

Date _____

Signature _____

To Learn

Activity J – Gears and More Gears

What are compound gears?

How can they be useful in designing and building gear trains?

Design a gear train:

- That has a ratio of at least 8:1 or 1:8.
- That contains at least one compound gear.

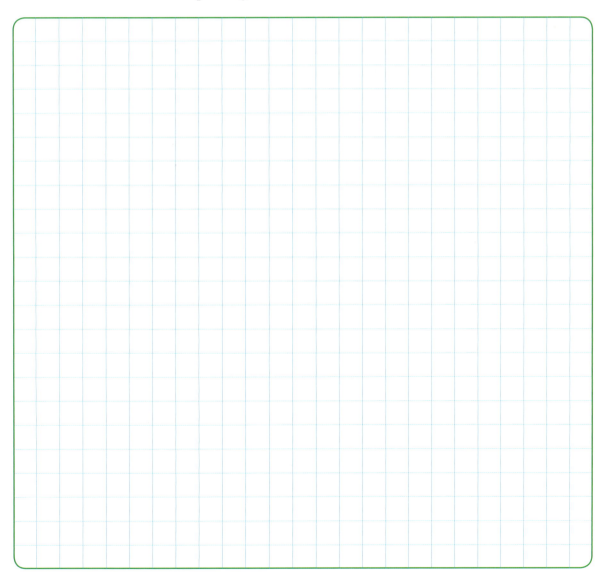

4-H Robotics:
Engineering for Today and Tomorrow
Robotics Notebook

Date _____

Signature _____

To Do

Activity K – Gear Train Design Team

Design Criteria:

- Must be powered by motor and battery.
- Must use gears to go slower.
- Must be able to propel a car (robot) to climb a cardboard ramp at an incline.

Describe how the gear train will work and propel a car up a ramp. Don't forget to mention the gear ratio and the different gears you will use.

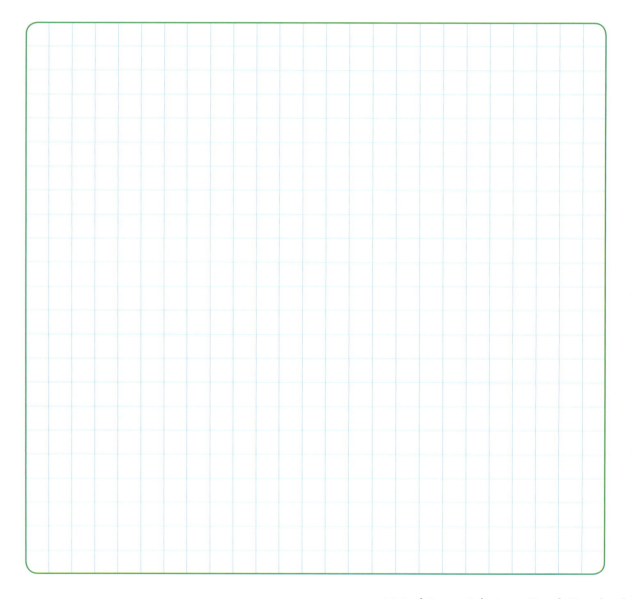

4-H Junk Drawer Robotics • **Youth Notebook**

Date _____

Signature _____

To Make

Activity L – Gear Train Build Team

Draw any changes you've made to your original design.

Record your final gear ratio.

How do compound gears help with creating a gear train?

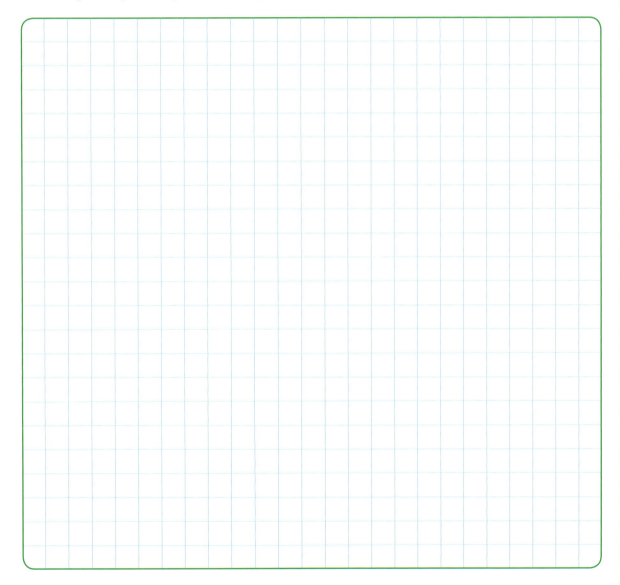

4-H Junk Drawer Robotics • Youth Notebook

4-H Robotics:
Engineering for Today and Tomorrow
Robotics Notebook

Date _____

Signature _____

To Do

Activity M – Es-Car-Go Design Team

Design a vehicle that:

- Is powered by motor and battery.
- Uses a drive train of gears.
- Moves slowly.
- Will climb an inclined cardboard ramp.

52

4-H Junk Drawer Robotics • Youth Notebook

4-H Robotics:
Engineering for Today and Tomorrow
Robotics Notebook

Date _____

Signature _____

To Make

Activity N — Es-Car-Go Build Team

Describe what you observed as you built the rover.

How did your robot and others use different types or amounts of parts?

What functions do the different parts of your robot serve?

While you were constructing your robot, did you have to change your design or alter any parts? Which ones and why?

4-H Junk Drawer Robotics • **Youth Notebook**   53

4-H Robotics:
Engineering for Today and Tomorrow
Robotics Notebook

Date _____

Signature _____

To Learn

Activity O – Pennies in a Boat

Design an aluminum foil boat to hold as many pennies as possible before sinking.

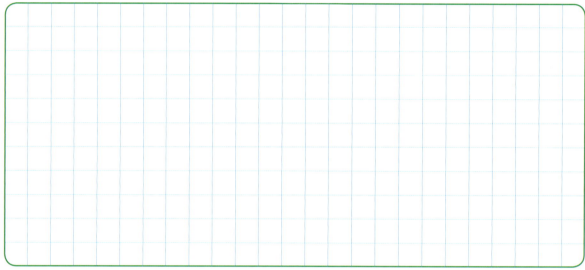

# of pennies held _____

Redesign your boat to improve its performance.

# of pennies held _____

What strategies worked to get more pennies in your boat?

Did you put the pennies on the same spot or spread them out?

Why do you think testing and then redesigning is important?

4-H Robotics:
Robotics Notebook

Date _____

Signature _____

To Learn

Activity P – Sink or Float

In the table, list items that you will test for buoyancy. Predict by putting check marks in the "float", "sink", or "I don't know" columns for each item. After you test the items, record the actual outcomes in the last column.

Item	Float	Sink	I Don't Know	Actual Results

How did you base your predictions, and how did they change after testing?

What similarities/differences are there in the items that floated and those that sank?

What item(s) did you try to make into a "flinker"? Why did or didn't it work?

4-H Junk Drawer Robotics • **Youth Notebook**   **55**

4-H Robotics:
Engineering for Today and Tomorrow
Robotics Notebook

CAREER CONNECTIONS

Career Connection 4: Iterative Design Process

Engineers use scientific knowledge to develop safe and economical solutions to real-world problems. When building these products, they follow a basic process of design and creation that is repeated and refined as they work to solve the problem. This repeating and refining is known as an iterative process. The first idea, design, or item is just one step to a final, more complete and developed solution, one step that is repeated over and over until the best results have been obtained.

When presented with a problem or an opportunity, an engineer will first ask questions. These questions help an engineer research a problem, constraints, and objectives. For example, engineers may ask, "What exactly is the problem? What have others done?" Such inquiries allow an engineer to define and state a problem.

Once engineers have identified a problem and researched its background, they begin to imagine the possibilities. They generate ideas and possible solutions. This creative process is essential to develop solutions.

After narrowing down their ideas, engineers evaluate and compare possible solutions so they can plan their next steps. Engineers often use notebooks to write lists of needed resources and draw diagrams of designs. They might also look for other people to help them. Cooperation is an important part of the engineering process. Next, engineers build their device. Using their plan, they use materials to physically craft their idea.

After engineers have a working model, they test and redesign the technology. Engineers know that there is always room for improvement. They communicate and discuss the results of their tests. They modify their device and retest it. This step in the process ensures that engineers create the best possible product.

Finally, engineers communicate the final product and share their solutions with others.

- How have you used an iterative process to solve a problem? Describe what you did.
- What are some products that you think need more iterations to make them better?
- How does iteration help an engineer design better products?

Adapted from the Engineering is Elementary project and Graphic Define on-line magazine (Issue 1 Iterative Design).

4-H Junk Drawer Robotics • **Youth Notebook**

4-H Robotics:
Engineering for Today and Tomorrow
Robotics Notebook

Date _____

Signature _____

To Do

Activity Q – Sea Hunt Design Team

Your underwater ROV must:

- Be designed to have neutral buoyancy.
- Have a tether for motor control.
- Be able to move up and down in a tank of water.

Below: Design your underwater ROV from the parts shown.

4-H Junk Drawer Robotics • Youth Notebook

4-H Robotics:
Engineering for Today and Tomorrow
Robotics Notebook

Date _____

Signature _____

To Make

Activity R – Sea Hunt Build Team

Build, then test.

> **Test your ROV**
>
> 1 Buoyancy - _____
>
> 2 Submerge - _____
>
> 3 Surface - _____

Describe how your ROV functioned in the water tank testing.

Use a deep container, garbage can, swimming pool, or other "test tank" to find out the performance of your ROV. Do water testing outdoors and have extra towels for cleanup.

List any improvements that can be made to your underwater ROV.

4-H Robotics:
Engineering for Today and Tomorrow
Robotics Notebook

Date _____

Signature _____

To Do

Activity 5 — To Make the Best Better
Design and Build Team

Your redesigned underwater ROV must meet these requirements:

- Be designed to have neutral buoyancy.
- Have a tether for motor control.
- Be able to move up and down.

Redesign your underwater ROV below.

What worked well with your redesigned ROV?

What helped you to improve your original design?

4-H Junk Drawer Robotics • Youth Notebook

59

4-H Robotics:
Engineering for Today and Tomorrow
Robotics Notebook

Robotics Notebook
Level 3

Mechatronics

In this level, you will learn about the internal components of a robot. You will learn how to build circuits, and how to write an effective program. These skills will allow you to create a robot of your choice.

Module 1 – Circuit Training

Module 1 will introduce you to the basics of electronic circuits. You will build your own circuits and explore different type of orientations and different types of switches. By the end of Module 1, you will create your own double pole double throw switch.

Module 2 – Come to Your Senses

In Module 2, you will learn how important sensors are to robots and the importance of accuracy. Module 2 will allow you to see the importance of accuracy and efficiency. At the end, you will build a car that can sense a wall and change direction to avoid crashing into the wall.

Module 3 – It's Logical

Module 3 will introduce to you the inner workings of a circuit. This module begins by teaching you a new way of counting called binary. You will then move on to logic gates, which help circuits make different decisions based on the information they receive. Toward the end of Module 3, you will begin building circuits on a prototyping board.

Module 4 – Do What I Say!

Module 4 will introduce you to programming and how computers operate. You will begin by following a computer program, acting out your specific role. Once the concept of programming is understood, you will develop a program for your group to perform.

Module 5 – Ready, SET, Go!

This final module is the conclusion of *Junk Drawer Robotics*. Here you will take all the knowledge you have developed through all the activities and design and create a robot combining many systems.

4-H Robotics:
Engineering for Today and Tomorrow
Robotics Notebook

Date _____

Signature _____

Electrical Circuits

There are many ways to create an electrical circuit for the flow of electricity (electrons) to do things like buzz a buzzer, or make a motor turn, or light a lamp bulb.

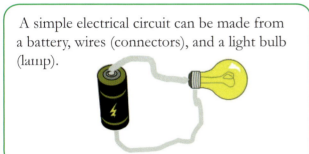

A simple electrical circuit can be made from a battery, wires (connectors), and a light bulb (lamp).

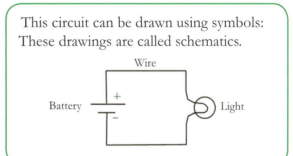

This circuit can be drawn using symbols: These drawings are called schematics.

Conductors and Insulators:

Most metals are good conductors of electricity. Copper and aluminum are some of the best and easily used conductors. Not all conductors are wire shaped; sometimes a metal frame or other part of a structure is used as part of a designed circuit. But be careful. If you don't want certain metal items as part of a circuit, you'll also need insulators to block the electrical flow in areas that you don't want electrons to go. Some good insulators are wood, rubber, or plastic. These insulators can be placed between, around, or covering a conductor to help direct where the electrical current will flow.

Make your own conductors: Use craft sticks with holes and cover (wrap) them with aluminum foil to create electrical connectors. Then use brads, paper clips, and mini lamp sockets to complete the circuits. Use masking tape and rubber bands to hold the connections and battery in place.

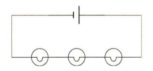

SERIES Circuit

A series circuit is one continuous loop from the battery, conductors, the bulbs, and then back to the battery.

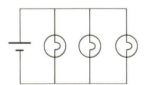

PARALLEL Circuit

A second way to set up a circuit is to have multiple paths or loops for the electrical flow from the battery. In a parallel circuit, each of the three lamps will have its own direct link to and from the battery.

Some circuits may have both "series" and "parallel" sections in the circuit. What do you think that circuit would look like?

4-H Junk Drawer Robotics • Youth Notebook

4-H Robotics:
Engineering for Today and Tomorrow
Robotics Notebook

Date _____

Signature _____

To Learn

Activity A – Series/Parallel

Step 1: Connect three lights in "series" so they are end to end. Describe or show below what worked.

Step 2: Connect three lights in "parallel" so they are in separate loops. Describe or show below what worked.

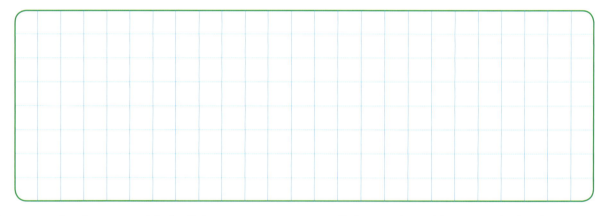

Compare what happens with the lights as you remove one light at a time. Also, note the brightness of the lights in each circuit: Are lights brighter in one circuit than the other?

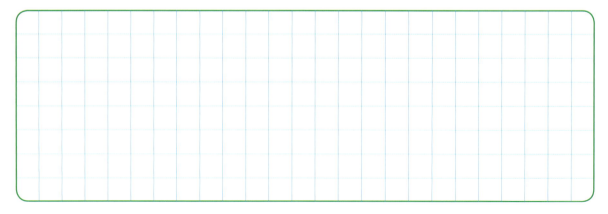

4-H Robotics:
Engineering for Today and Tomorrow
Robotics Notebook

Date _____

Signature _____

Electrical Switches

The electrical flow in a circuit may need to have a control to turn it on and off. The use of a switch or switches can provide ease of control while retaining good contacts at the connections. A number of different types of switches can be made in a circuit.

Single Pole Single Throw (On/Off) Switch (SPST):

The simplest switch is a single pole single throw switch; it will open and close one circuit.

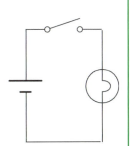

Double Pole Single Throw Switch (DPST):

This switch can operate two circuits at the same time, opening and closing them together. It is like two single pole switches next to each other.

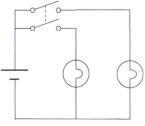

Single Pole Double Throw Switch (SPDT):

This type of switch can control two different circuits, one at a time. One circuit can be opened as a second circuit is closed.

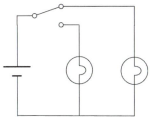

Double Pole Double Throw Switch (DPDT):

This switch can operate two circuits at the same time, opening and closing them together. It is like two single pole switches next to each other.

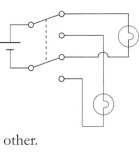

Simple switches can be made with craft sticks with holes, aluminum foil, paper clips, and brass brads. Here are some designs for DPDT switches. What design can you create for a switch?

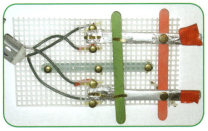

4-H Junk Drawer Robotics • Youth Notebook   63

4-H Robotics:
Engineering for Today and Tomorrow
Robotics Notebook

Date _____

Signature _____

To Learn

Activity B – Off and On

Challenge 1: Make a singe pole switch to control the lights in the "series" circuit you made in Activity A. Describe or show below how it worked.

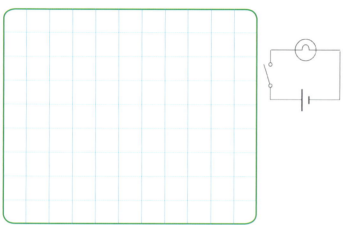

Challenge 2: Make a singe pole switch to control just one of the lights in the "parallel" circuit you made in Activity A. Describe or show below how it works.

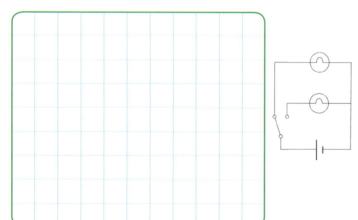

Challenge 3: Make a singe pole **double throw** switch to control two different lights one at a time. Describe or show below how it works.

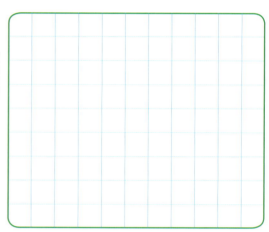

- Which type of switch is the easiest to make? The hardest? Why?
- How could different designs of switches be beneficial to the circuit?
- Is there a way to turn the light on and off without touching the switch?

4-H Junk Drawer Robotics • **Youth Notebook**

4-H Robotics:
Engineering for Today and Tomorrow
Robotics Notebook

Date _____

Signature _____

To Learn

Activity C – Direction of Flow

Step 1: Build a circuit with a battery, wires, and a motor. Attach something to the motor shaft to help determine the direction of rotation. Once you know the rotation, explore how to change or reverse the rotation. Describe how you changed direction of the rotation.

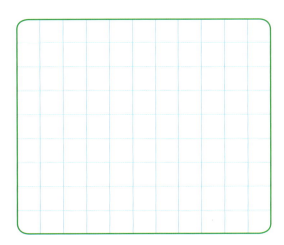

Step 2: Use the parallel circuit made in Activity A and replace one of the holiday mini lights with a mini LED light, if available. Record observations and then change the battery connection in the circuit. Again record observations. How did the lights respond? Were they on in either position? If not, how would you explain this?

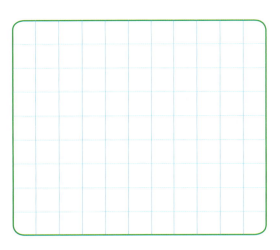

Compare how the changes in the direction of the electrical flow affected the lights, the motor, and the LEDs. How would this affect your robot's movement and design?

4-H Junk Drawer Robotics • Youth Notebook

65

4-H Robotics:
Engineering for Today and Tomorrow
Robotics Notebook

Date _____

Signature _____

To Do

Activity D – Forward and Reverse Design Team

The challenge is to design a switch that will do the following:

- Must be able to switch the + and - battery power direction to the motor.
- Must be able to reverse the direction of the motor with one switch motion.

Hint: Consider a type of double pole double throw (DPDT) switch.

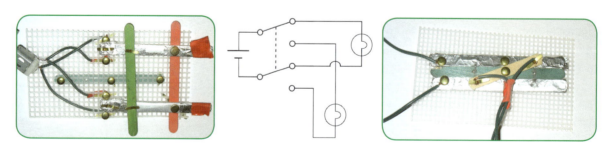

4-H Junk Drawer Robotics • Youth Notebook

Date _____

Signature _____

To Make

Activity E – Forward and Reverse Build Team

Draw your final design below. Indicate any changes that you made after testing.

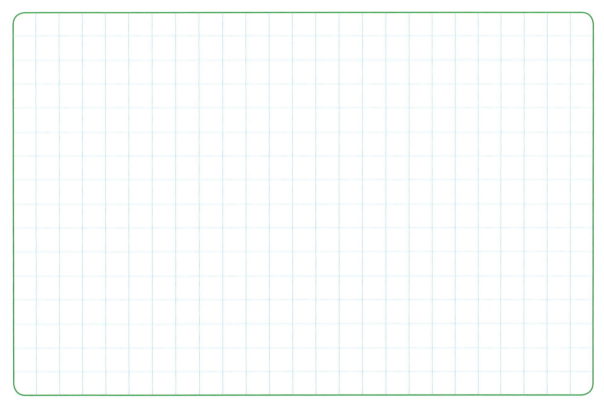

Try adding a tether (long cable wires) so that you can control a motor from a distance. Can you use this remote switch to control your Es-Car-Go or Sea Hunt ROV from Level 2, Robots on the Move?

What changes did you make to your original design?

What is another way to operate the switch? (e.g., syringes, electricity, motors)

4-H Robotics:
Engineering for Today and Tomorrow
Robotics Notebook

CAREER CONNECTIONS

Using Nature as an Inspiration

Engineers use science and math in order to develop safe and useful solutions to real-world problems. So where do engineers get the ideas for these creations? Often, they simply look out their window!

We live in an incredible natural world. Earth has a wonderful natural environment with highly adapted animals and plants. The arms, eyes, wings, and leaves of plants and animals have been functioning for centuries. These highly developed designs have already solved some of the problems humans are struggling with, and they serve as inspirations for engineers. Almost all engineering products imitate some aspect of nature. This idea is called "biomimicry."

For example, owls were the basis for military planes that are undetectable by radar. The locative abilities of the bat led to mobile robots with their own guidance systems. Butterflies with fluorescent wings helped redesign LED lights. The super strength of spider webs enabled sturdier materials and building designs. Red seaweed inspired resistant antibiotics.

As you can see, engineers have a whole world of natural phenomenon to study! Creatures, plants, and geography help engineers satisfy our human needs. Nature serves as a model, mentor, and measure for engineers.

- Can you think of any products in your home that may have been modeled after an aspect of nature?
- Think of a plant, animal, or location. What natural mechanisms do they have that could be useful for humans?

Adapted from: http://www.biomimicryinstitute.org/

4-H Robotics:
Engineering for Today and Tomorrow
Robotics Notebook

Date _____

Signature _____

To Learn

Activity F – Line Follower

Senses

What are some of our senses?

What senses could a robot have?

After using a couple of "binoculars" with different spacing to follow the tape line, draw a representation of the lines made by the markers.

Compare how the lines differ and describe how accuracy and precision can be an important factor.

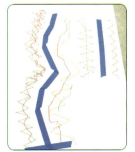
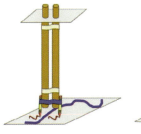
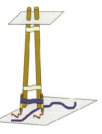

4-H Junk Drawer Robotics • Youth Notebook

69

4-H Robotics:
Engineering for Today and Tomorrow
Robotics Notebook

Date _____

Signature _____

To Learn

Activity G – Keep in Touch

Reading Braille takes practice and skill. Take turns to feel the code of bumps. Record the locations and spacing and then chart the results.

Once you have recorded the dots, use the chart to decode the letters and discover the word coded in Braille.

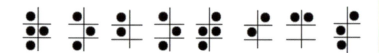

Processor Code deciphering area for Braille letters and words

Draw dots where *"sensor"* indicates for each letter. Do one word, then use the code chart to de-code letters one at a time and tell *"output"* the letter. Repeat for the next word.

1.

2.

3.

Output

"Output" write down letters when told by *"processor."*

Decode the chart using the alphabet chart above.

1. _____ _____ _____ _____ _____

2. _____ _____ _____ _____ _____

3. _____ _____ _____ _____ _____

70

4-H Junk Drawer Robotics • Youth Notebook

4-H Robotics:
Engineering for Today and Tomorrow
Robotics Notebook

Date _____

Signature _____

To Learn

Activity H – Don't Buzz Me

Have team members play the roles of
1. a timer,
2. a recorder, and
3. a tester.

Move a looped wand to follow the live wire without buzzing.

Compare the results and discuss precision, accuracy, and sensitivity.

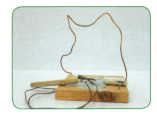

Don't Buzz Me!

Use the chart to record the results of sensitivity using two different size loops or hooks on the wire game.

Repeat three times for an average.

Record the number of Buzzes and the overall time to pass the loop from one end of the wire to the other end.

Person and loop size	Number of buzzes		Time to complete
	Buzz marks	Total	Time
Name / large loop			
1			
2			
3			
average			
Name / small loop			
1			
2			
3			
average			

4-H Junk Drawer Robotics • Youth Notebook

4-H Robotics:
Engineering for Today and Tomorrow
Robotics Notebook

Date _____

Signature _____

To Do

Activity 1 – Wall Following Design Team

Design Criteria:

- The client wants a robot that can follow or track around an item or wall on its own without direct control.
- The client wants a simple robot that can be made from recycled cups, craft sticks, containers, or other small cartons.
- A battery pack, two motors with small direct drive wheels/tires, and a sensor trigger switch should be common supplies to make/use.

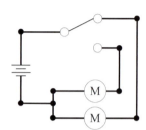

Use or modify a circuit using a SPDT switch to create a wall follower.

Draw your robot designs below:

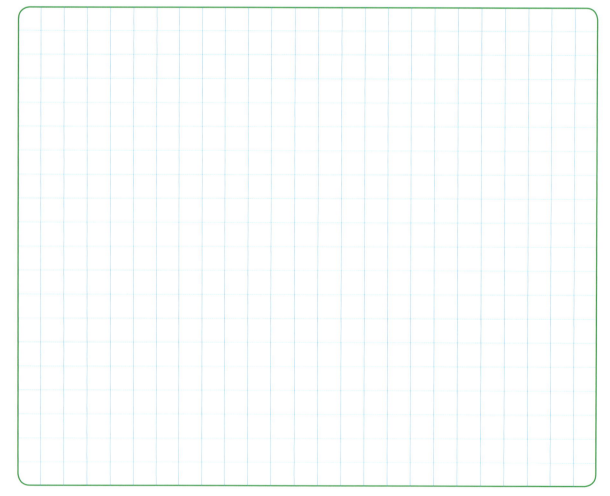

72 4-H Junk Drawer Robotics • Youth Notebook

4-H Robotics:
Engineering for Today and Tomorrow
Robotics Notebook

Date _____

Signature _____

To Make

Activity J – Wall Following Build Team

Explain how your circuit works and how the sensor works.

How did your robot move and follow the wall?

Draw your final design below:

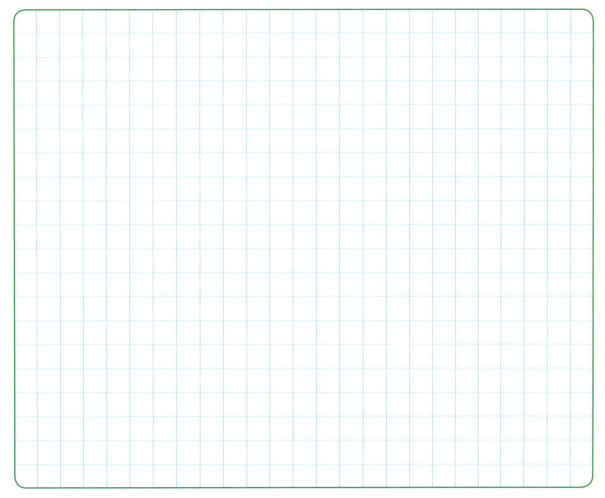

4-H Junk Drawer Robotics • Youth Notebook

4-H Robotics:
Engineering for Today and Tomorrow
Robotics Notebook

Date _____

Signature _____

To Learn

Activity K – It's About Time

What are some of the advantages and disadvantages of binary counting versus base 10?

How do you think computers and other electronic systems use this binary (base 2) counting system?

How often do you think the computer needs to check for new data? Why is this important? How might this impact a robot and its actions?

Binary (0111) = Base 10 (7)
as these youth act out "1's and 0's."

4-H Robotics:
Engineering for Today and Tomorrow
Robotics Notebook

Date _____

Signature _____

To Learn

Activity L – Logic: AND, OR, NOT!

Logic Gates

The basic logic gates used in binary and electrical circuits include the following symbols and truth tables: Truth tables are listings of all the possible options for the logic in each setting. The table is composed of a column for each input and a column for the output.

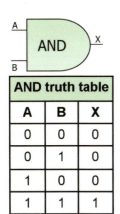
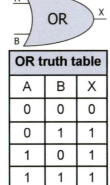
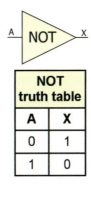

Combination Gates

What would the truth tables look like for the NAND and NOR gates?

How are they different from the AND and OR gates?

Fill out the truth tables for NAND and NOR after completing the main activity on logic circuits.

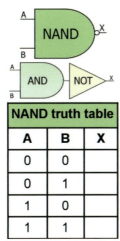
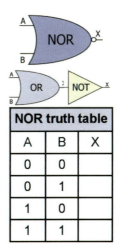

4-H Junk Drawer Robotics • Youth Notebook

75

4-H Robotics:
Engineering for Today and Tomorrow
Robotics Notebook

Date _____

Signature _____

To Learn

Activity L – Logic: AND, OR, NOT!

How many different ways are there to get the desired output?

What would happen if you used three or more input points?

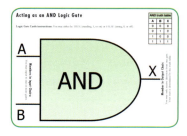

4-H Robotics:
Engineering for Today and Tomorrow
Robotics Notebook

Date _____

Signature _____

Using logic gates to provide digital outputs

In the sample activity on the right, an analog input, such as rising temperature, turns on the switches at certain points as the temperatures are reached. This is recorded electronically and shown in the digital states of the outputs.

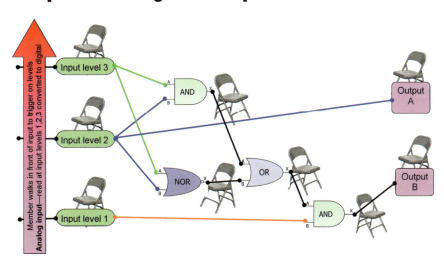

The four graphics on the left illustrate the four states for the temperature reading above.

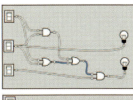

Cold reading, no switch on and both lights off (binary 00 = 0).

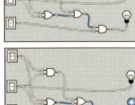

Second is a cool reading with one switch on and one light on (binary 01 = 1).

Next is a warm reading with two switches on and the other light on (binary 10 = 2).

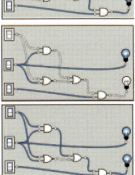

This graphic shows hot with three switches on and both lights on (binary 11 = 3).

Notice how the output lights from the temperature circuit could also be used as indicators of temperature in a digital thermometer, or how the outputs could be connected to the inputs of the "position control" logic circuits as shown on the right.

Why might the outputs from the position control be better to indicate the different temperatures?

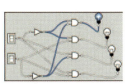
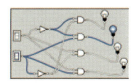

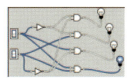

4-H Junk Drawer Robotics • **Youth Notebook**

77

4-H Robotics:
Engineering for Today and Tomorrow
Robotics Notebook

Date _____

Signature _____

To Learn

Activity M – Analog Versus Digital

What is analog data? What is digital data? Which works better and why?

Where have you seen an analog to digital converter?

What other things might use a similar logic circuit like the ones you acted out?

What would have to change for it to work?

4-H Robotics:
Engineering for Today and Tomorrow
Robotics Notebook

Date _____

Signature _____

Components

Battery

A battery is used to provide direct current (DC) to the circuit. Batteries come in several different sizes and shapes. Some of the common batteries are AA, C, D, and 9 volt.

Resistor

A resistor restricts the flow of current in a circuit to a set value. Resistors are not polarized and can be placed in a circuit in any direction.

Capacitor

A capacitor stores the current in a circuit, and then releases the current once the capacitor is filled. The capacitor will continue to repeat this process as long as the circuit is complete and a current is flowing. Capacitors are polarized and will only work if connected correctly.

Diodes

A diode restricts the flow in a current in a single direction. Diodes are polarized and must be placed in a circuit in the correct direction.

LED

A light emitting diode, also known as an LED, is a special diode that produces a light when current passes through. LEDs are polarized and will not light if placed in an incorrect orientation. There is usually a notch or flat side on the LED to mark the cathode (negative) side.

Wires

Wires are used to carry current in a circuit. Wires are made of a conductive material, usually copper. Wires come in different sizes and are measured by diameters and units of AWG (American Wire Gauge).

Switch

Switches are used to open and close a circuit. There are several different types of switches, which are named by the amount of poles and throws they have, for example, a Single Pole Single Throw switch. A pole is the number of circuits to control, and a throw is the number of circuit paths that are controllable.

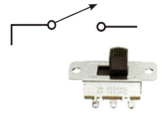

4-H Robotics:
Engineering for Today and Tomorrow
Robotics Notebook

Date_____

Signature_____

To Make

Activity N – Components

In an electrical current, what could the ping-pong balls represent?

In your own words, describe how each individual component works.

What do the balls that fall on the floor represent?

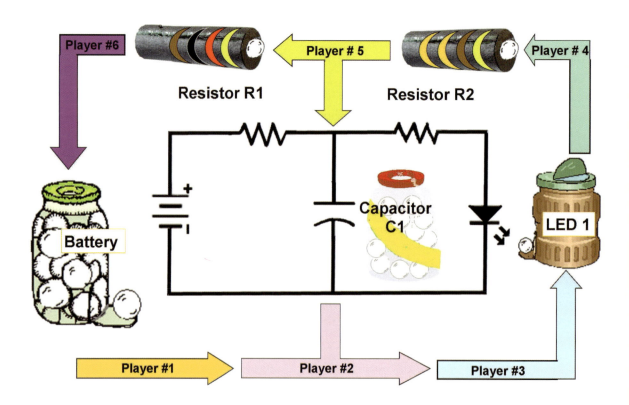

80   4-H Junk Drawer Robotics • Youth Notebook

4-H Robotics:
Engineering for Today and Tomorrow
Robotics Notebook

Date _____

Signature _____

Using Breadboards and Components

Each team will receive one circuit description, **schematic**, and instructions to create a sample circuit to highlight how electronic circuits work.

Additional and more advanced circuits can be made using electronics kits and components for those who want to do more in this area.

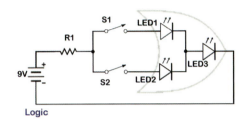

A **Breadboard** is a tool to test circuit designs by allowing components, wires, and power to be set up, and the logic tried out and verified before building the permanent circuit and structure. A breadboard is made up of rows and columns of holes connected in groups. The components can be pushed into the holes and temporary connections can be made for testing. Breadboards makes it easier to move, replace, or add other connections or components.

How to Read a Resistor

The 1st band signifies the tens place. The 2nd band signifies the ones place. The 3rd band signifies how much to multiply by, and the 4th band represents the tolerance or variation of resistance.

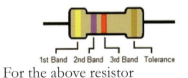

COLOR	1st BAND	2nd BAND	3rd BAND/ MULTIPLIER	4th BAND/ TOLERANCE
Black	0	0	1Ω	
Brown	1	1	10Ω	
Red	2	2	100Ω	
Orange	3	3	1KΩ	
Yellow	4	4	10KΩ	
Green	5	5	100KΩ	
Blue	6	6	1MΩ	
Violet	7	7	10MΩ	
Gray	8	8		
White				
Gold				± 5%
Silver				± 10%

For the above resistor

Band 1st	2nd	3rd	4th
Yellow,	Violet,	Red,	Gold
4	7	100Ω	±5%

The resistor value is 4700 Ω ± 5%

Can also be written as 4.7K Ω ± 5%.

The 5 percent tolerance means it has a range of 4465 Ω to 4935 Ω.

Here are some other common resistors. Can you figure out the resistance?

Red   Red   Brown   Gold
_____   _____ X _____ ± _____
Band 1 Band 2   Band 3   Band 4

Orange Orange Green   Silver
_____   _____ X _____ ± _____
Band 1 Band 2   Band 3   Band 4

4-H Junk Drawer Robotics • Youth Notebook

81

4-H Robotics:
Engineering for Today and Tomorrow
Robotics Notebook

Date _____

Signature _____

To Make

Activity O – Breadboard Build Team

Draw your wire diagram below. Don't forget to record the values of all resistors, capacitors, and diodes.

Take notes on how other circuits function.

4-H Robotics:
Engineering for Today and Tomorrow
Robotics Notebook

Date _____

Signature _____

CAREER CONNECTIONS

Engineering Professions

Engineers develop solutions to problems in every aspect of life. However, it would be impractical for each engineer to know a lot about everything, so engineers specialize in a field of engineering, such as electricity, civil, medicine, machines, chemistry, or robotics.

There are almost 300,000 electrical engineers in the United States designing electronic equipment. They are responsible for a wide range of technology and often specialize in a specific area, like robot control systems. Electronic engineers provide technologies such as GPS and automobile wiring.

Civil engineering is considered one of the oldest branches of engineering. The basic duties of civil engineers are design and construction of bridges, roads, buildings, dams, and other structures. While some civil engineers manage large scale projects, others do research on improving materials or designs.

Biomedical engineers combine engineering with biological and medical concepts. They develop devices and procedures that solve health-related problems, such as artificial organs. Many biomedical engineers do research on the relation of engineering and the human body, finding robotic replacements for limbs.

Industrial engineers determine the most effective ways for companies to use basic components like people, machines, and information. They are interested in increasing efficiency and productivity, so they devise management and production systems.

Mechanical engineers design and manufacture machines, engines, tools, and other mechanical devices. They develop machines that produce power, such as generators and turbines, and machines that use power, such as air conditioners and elevators.

Although these engineering professions focus on different fields, they share many commonalities. All engineers follow a similar design process. They use notebooks to record their findings, and they test and retest their devices. Ultimately, all engineers use critical thinking to devise solutions for everyday problems. Engineers in different fields work together and combine their knowledge to create the best possible outcomes.

- Which engineering career best fits your interests?
- Which engineering fields are involved in designing and building robots?

4-H Robotics:
Engineering for Today and Tomorrow
Robotics Notebook

Date _____

Signature _____

To Learn

Activity P – Cashier

Shopper	Input	Processor	Output
Will show the input of a barcode and await further instructions from output	Will read the barcode, and will tell the processor the barcode number	Will take in the barcode number and search for the item. Processor will tell output of the item and price or that the product does not exist	Will take in the information from the processor, write item and price on a chart, and go "beep" or "err" if product does not exist

Can any of the steps be broken down into more steps?

Are there any shortcuts that can be made to speed up the process?

What are some examples of real life control systems?

What kind of control system do human have?

84 4-H Junk Drawer Robotics • Youth Notebook

4-H Robotics:
Engineering for Today and Tomorrow
Robotics Notebook

Date _____

Signature _____

Flowchart Elements

Terminal – used to show an action, such as start or stop, in a program.

Input/Output – represents the acquisition of information or the telling of data.

Process – used to represent a general process, like a change in value, location, or form of data.

Decision – used to show how choices can cause branches or loops as alternate paths.

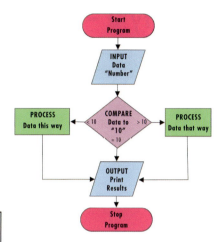

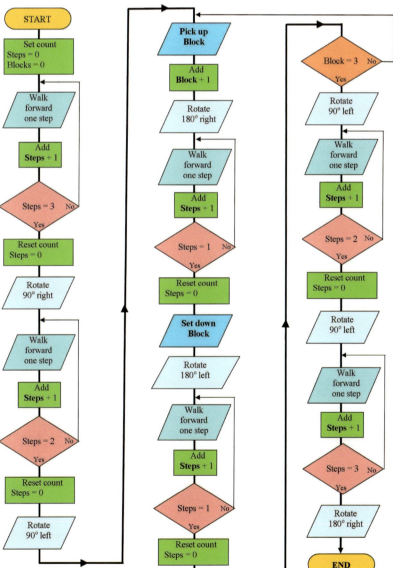

A computer program is basically instructions that the computer can understand and follow.

The program language will have "grammar" or syntax on how and what can be written for the computer to understand.

Above are sample ideas and elements that are found in a simple flowchart used as the basis for the writing a program in a specific language.

On the left is a flowchart to be acted out by a team of three to four young people.

4-H Junk Drawer Robotics • Youth Notebook

4-H Robotics:
Engineering for Today and Tomorrow
Robotics Notebook

Date _____

Signature _____

To Learn

Activity Q – Walk the Walk

Actuator	Processor	Data Memory
Motion control and movement (input and output)	Reading instructions, making decisions, giving feedback	Doing math and keeping count of number of steps and blocks during activity

What are ways to improve the program/flowchart?

Is this the most efficient way to run a program/flowchart? If not, how can the program be more efficient?

How would you program a robot to perform a certain task, including sensors?

4-H Robotics:
Engineering for Today and Tomorrow
Robotics Notebook

Date _____

Signature _____

To Do

Activity R – Say What? Design Team

What is the objective of your program/flowchart?

What instruction do you want the program to follow?

What loops can be incorporated into your program/flowchart?

4-H Robotics:
Engineering for Today and Tomorrow
Robotics Notebook

Date _____

Signature _____

To Make

Activity S – Say What? Build Team

Are there any problems with the program you have been given?

How accurate and precise is the program?

What changes can you make to the program? (debug, less steps, simpler)

What changes have been made to your program?

4-H Robotics:
Engineering for Today and Tomorrow
Robotics Notebook

Date _____

Signature _____

You will design and create your own robot

As a scientist, an engineer, and a technologist, you have explored and experienced many parts of robotics systems and processes. Now that you have explored the world of robotics, you are ready to use what you have learned and acquired from the *Junk Drawer Robotics* activities.

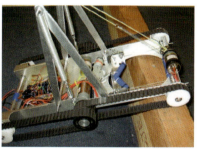

Your Robotics Notebook should have lots of information and ideas that you have created and that you can use to develop and create a robot of your own design and capability. You can take what you have learned about power sources of electricity and pneumatics to power your robot. You can take information on the movement of robot arms and apply this to the work that your robot will do. You can devise transmission of power using gear trains, levers, and linkages for movement. You know the elements in programming and simple sensors to add control to your robot.

Review your notes and comments in your notebook to help you as you put together the many systems in a robot just for you.

You are free to design a robot in any way that you like because you know much more about what works and what designs will be able to be constructed into a robot.

Some ideas that you may want to consider:

- Do you want a robot vehicle?
- A robot to explore the land or underwater environment?
- A robot to sense its surroundings and respond in some manner?

You may want to try other *4-H Robotics: Engineering for Today and Tomorrow* curriculum such as *Virtual Robotics* or *Robotics Platforms* to do different things and experience different levels of interaction.

In addition, many books and materials can provide more ideas and suggestions. You may want to use building sets such as K'nex® or LEGO®. Homemade robots also can be created in various ways using other hardware store supplies or household materials.

Good luck.

4-H Junk Drawer Robotics • Youth Notebook

4-H Robotics:
Engineering for Today and Tomorrow
Robotics Notebook

Date _____

Signature _____

To Do

Activity T – Build Your Own Robot Design Team

What is the objective of your robot?

Design your robot below:

90   4-H Junk Drawer Robotics • **Youth Notebook**